Communicating Today

The Internet and email

love your library

Buckinghamshire Libraries
0845 230 3232

www.buckscc.gov.uk/libraries

---

24 hour renewal line
0303 123 0035

www.heinemann.co.uk/library
Visit our website to find out more information about **Heinemann Library** books.

To order:
☎ Phone ++44 (0)1865 888066
📠 Send a fax to ++44 (0)1865 314091
💻 Visit the Heinemann Bookshop at www.heinemann.co.uk/library to browse our catalogue and order online.

First published in Great Britain by Heinemann Library, Halley Court, Jordan Hill, Oxford OX2 8EJ, a division of Reed Educational and Professional Publishing Ltd. Heinemann is a registered trademark of Reed Educational & Professional Publishing Ltd.

OXFORD MELBOURNE AUCKLAND JOHANNESBURG BLANTYRE
GABORONE IBADAN PORTSMOUTH NH (USA) CHICAGO

© Reed Educational and Professional Publishing Ltd 2001
The moral right of the proprietor has been asserted.

All rights reserved. No part of this publication may be reproduced, stored in a retrieval system, or transmitted in any form or by any means, electronic, mechanical, photocopying, recording, or otherwise without either the prior written permission of the Publishers or a licence permitting restricted copying in the United Kingdom issued by the Copyright Licensing Agency Ltd, 90 Tottenham Court Road, London W1P 0LP.

Designed by Visual Image
Illustrations by Visual Image
Originated by Ambassador Litho Ltd.
Printed in Hong Kong/China

06 05 04 03 02   06 05 04 03 02
10 9 8 7 6 5 4 3 2   10 9 8 7 6 5 4 3 2 1
ISBN 0431 11375 0 (hardback)   ISBN 0431 11382 3 (paperback)

British Library Cataloguing in Publication Data

Oxlade, Chris
   Internet and e-mail. – (Communicating today)
   1. Internet – Juvenile literature
   2. Electronic mail systems – Juvenile literature
   I. Title
   004.6'78

BUCKS COUNTY LIBRARIES	
PET	549286
J004.678	24-Mar-06
£6.75	

Acknowledgements

The Publishers would like to thank the following for permission to reproduce photographs:
Associated Press Photos: p10; Bob Battersby: p13; Borders: p24; Bush Internet: p11; Corbis: pp6, 28, Commander John Leenhouts p29; Earthlink: p8; Google: p21; Microsoft: pp14, 16, 17; NASA: p20; R.D. Battersby: p12; San Diego Zoo: p22; Sega: p26; Stockbyte: p23; Stone: p4, Hunter Freeman p18, Walter Hodges p5, Steven Peters p27; The Stock Market: p15; Trevor Clifford: p9; WWF: p19.

Cover photograph reproduced with permission of Stone.

Every effort has been made to contact copyright holders of any material reproduced in this book. Any omissions will be rectified in subsequent printings if notice is given to the Publisher.

CONTENTS

What are communications? **4**

Connecting computers **6**

Getting on the Internet **8**

Connection devices **10**

Electronic mail **12**

Sending an e-mail **14**

Getting an e-mail **16**

The World Wide Web **18**

Surfing the Web **20**

Through the Internet **22**

Building a website **24**

Internet news and chat **26**

Internet timeline **28**

Glossary **30**

Index **32**

Any words appearing in the text in bold, **like this**, are explained in the Glossary.

WHAT ARE COMMUNICATIONS?

Communications are ways of sending and receiving information. Important ones include television, radio, telephone (and fax) the Internet (and e-mail), post and newspapers.

This book is about the Internet – what it is, and how people use it. It looks at the technology and science involved, how information is created and sent through the Internet, and the people who operate it.

What is the Internet?

You may have used the Internet yourself. Even if you haven't, you will almost certainly have heard a lot about it. It is the newest form of telecommunications, and it has created a revolution in communications since the mid-1990s.

The Internet is part of everyday life for many children today. They use it at home and school for research, homework and entertainment.

The Internet is an electronic communication system that connects millions of computers in hundreds of countries around the world, and allows **data** (information stored on the computers) to move between them. Many of the computers connected to the Internet belong to businesses, schools, governments and other big organizations. But many also belong to families like yours, who use the Internet to communicate with friends, for research, education, shopping, hobbies, or just for fun.

The Internet makes it as easy and cheap to communicate between places on different continents as it is to communicate between places in the same town. Because of this, the Internet can make the world seem a smaller place.

Using the Internet

The Internet has two main functions. The first is e-mail, which allows one Internet user to send a message to another Internet user. The second is the **World Wide Web**, which is a gigantic library of information stored on computers on the Internet. As it explains the Internet, this book looks at how an e-mail is sent and received and how people access information on a typical site on the World Wide Web.

People can buy thousands of different things over the Internet. This is called **on-line shopping**. They can also do **on-line banking**.

CONNECTING COMPUTERS

The Internet is a computer **network**. A network is made up of computers linked together so that they can share **data**. The simplest network is made up of two computers linked together by a wire.

The Internet network

Internet is short for 'international network'. The Internet already connects together millions of different computers in hundreds of different countries, and it is growing at astonishing speed. The number of computers on it is doubling approximately every year. By 2010, there could be a thousand million people using it!

Servers

On a small network, there is one computer, called a **server**, that holds all the data that the other computers (which are often called terminals) share. If a computer on the network needs some data, it sends an electronic request to the server, which sends the data back. A server is normally a powerful computer with huge storage capacity on its **hard drive**.

The Internet is made up of many thousands of servers, each with its own network connected to it. So you could think of the Internet as a network of networks.

There are computer networks within most offices like this one. Communication across the business is made easier and e-mails make sure that everyone stays in touch.

Network connections

Computers in the same room or building are connected by wires plugged into the computers, and sometimes by wireless **infra-red links** or radio links.

The servers on the Internet are connected together by high-speed, high-capacity communication lines, made up of **optical fibres** or **satellite** links. Some are the same lines that carry telephone calls; others are used only by the Internet. Some lines, such as the ones between the USA and Asia, carry a huge amount of data. They are like data motorways, and are known as the Internet's 'backbone'.

The Internet is not owned by anybody, but it is operated by the people and companies that run its servers and the telecommunications companies that operate the communication lines. They are called **Internet Service Providers** or ISPs (see page 8). There are also international organizations such as the Internet Society that agree the standard forms in which information should move around the Internet.

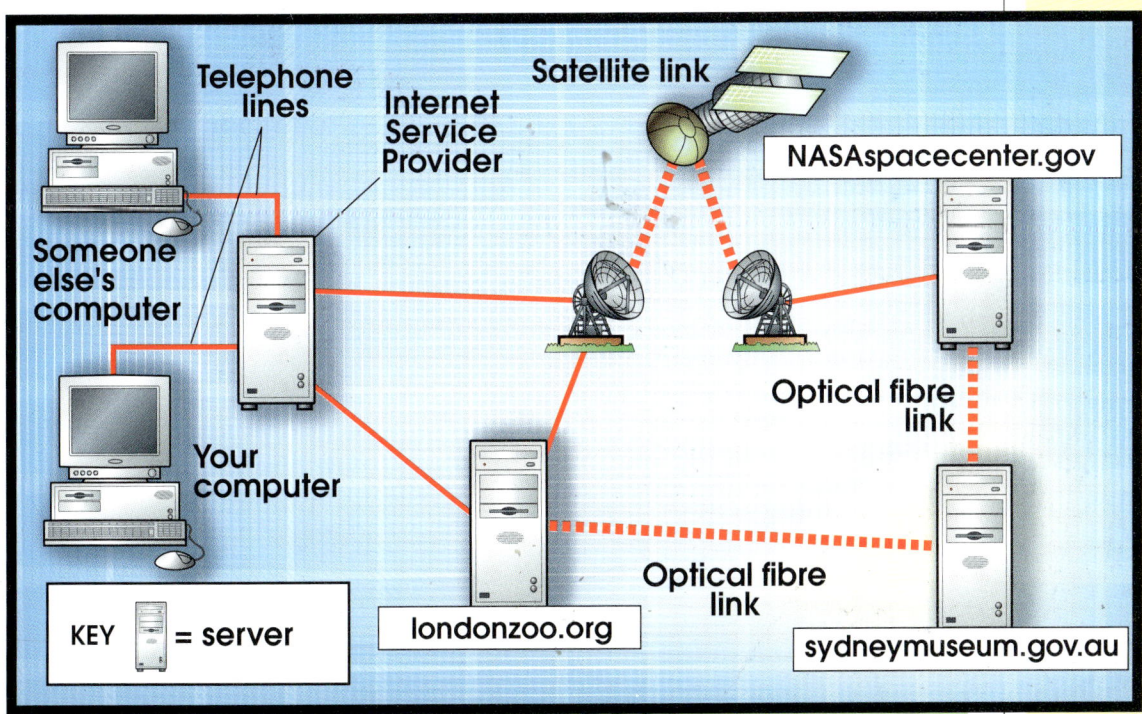

This network is linked in several different ways. Servers thousands of kilometres apart can send information to each other using this network. They close the link when they have sent or received the data they need.

GETTING ON THE INTERNET

The Internet's **server** computers are switched on and connected together day and night. The **data** on them is available to other computers on the Internet at any time.

Connections

Most Internet users have temporary connections, called dial-up connections. They connect their computers to one of the Internet's servers by telephone line. When their connection is working, they are said to be **on-line**. When they are disconnected, they are said to be **off-line**.

Organizations that operate servers that people can connect to are called **Internet Service Providers** (or ISPs). They provide a way into the Internet, and so they are called gateways. Some ISPs charge a monthly fee for being on-line, others are free. In countries where making phone calls to the ISP is free, such as the USA, people often stay on-line all day.

This is the home page of an Internet Service Provider (ISP). You can see all the different services that the ISP offers, including building your own website.

Modems

To connect to the Internet through a telephone line, you need a **modem**. The word 'modem' is short for modulator/demodulator. A modem converts (or modulates) **digital** signals from a computer into **analogue** signals that can travel along a telephone line. It also converts (demodulates) analogue signals from the telephone line back into computer data. The speed of a modem is measured in bits per second (bps), which is the amount of data that can go through it every second. The fastest standard modems work at 56 **kilobytes** per second (Kbps).

Some Internet users have digital connections to their Internet Service Providers called **ADSL** or **ISDN** lines. They allow data to travel much faster than telephone lines. They do not need modems to connect them to computers, but they do need other specialized **hardware**. In the future, all connections will be digital.

A modem that connects a personal computer to a domestic telephone line. This is called an external (rather than an internal) modem because it is outside the computer's case.

Analogue and digital

The signals that travel down most phone lines from telephones to telephone exchanges are called analogue signals. This means that the electric current is constantly getting stronger and weaker. Digital signals do not get stronger and weaker. They simply swap between being on or off, and are used to represent the binary digits 0 and 1. Digital signals are used in computers to show data in binary form.

CONNECTION DEVICES

Most people connect to the Internet from a personal computer on a desk at home or at work. But if you have a portable computer, a **modem** and a mobile phone which can handle **data**, you can connect to the Internet from almost anywhere. Palm-top computers and **personal digital assistants** (or PDAs) can access the Internet in the same way. Many other electronic devices can connect to the Internet, too.

Internet phones

Some telephones contain computers with **software** that can access the Internet. They have a small screen where you can write and read e-mails, and look at the **World Wide Web**. Mobile phones with a system called **Wireless Access Protocol** (WAP) can access the Internet, too, but they can only display text pages specially designed to be viewed on their small screens.

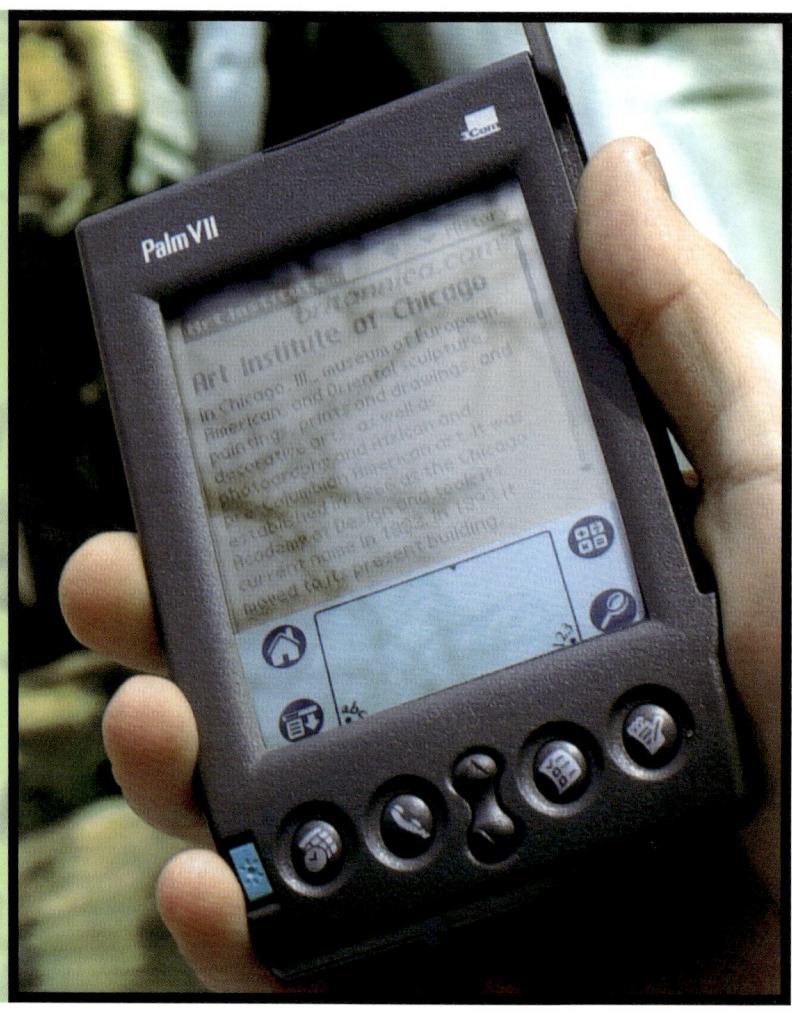

This is a palm-held computer. It can store thousands of names, addresses and notes. It can also send and receive e-mails and show **web pages**.

Internet on television

Some digital television systems, where the television signals are broadcast in digital form (such as digital **satellite** systems and digital **cable** systems), allow access to the Internet on television. They use a device that sits on top of the TV, called a 'set-top' box. Data comes from the **Internet Service Provider** (ISP) to the user's television via the satellite or cable. It gets from the user to the ISP along a telephone line. Some games consoles, such as the Sega Dreamcast, can also access the Internet, which means that players can play against each other **on-line**.

Convergence

At the start of the 1990s, most communication systems were separate from each other. You needed a television to watch television programmes, a telephone to make telephone calls, and a computer to access the Internet. Now, these systems are joining together. You can get the Internet on a television, and make phone calls over the Internet. Soon you will be able to get television on a phone over the Internet! This process of systems linking up is called convergence. Eventually, every home will probably have a single box that handles all its communication needs.

This TV shows the Internet too. As the barriers come down between different methods of communication new possibilities open up. Imagine the changes that may lie ahead in only the next few years!

ELECTRONIC MAIL

Electronic mail is always shortened to e-mail. For two people connected to the Internet, sending an e-mail is a quick and easy way of communicating. An e-mail arrives at its destination just a few seconds after it is sent, whether it is going to a computer next door or to one on the other side of the world. You can send the same message automatically to any number of people at the same time, too.

E-mail software

To send and receive e-mails, you need a computer with e-mail **software**. The software allows you to write e-mail messages, add the address of the person you are sending the message to, and send the message. It also lets you collect e-mails from your electronic **mailbox** and read them. Most e-mail programs also allow you to send **attachments**, such as picture **files**, that travel along with the e-mail.

E-mails like this one have made communication between people quicker and easier than it has ever been. You need to remember to check your e-mail regularly, though.

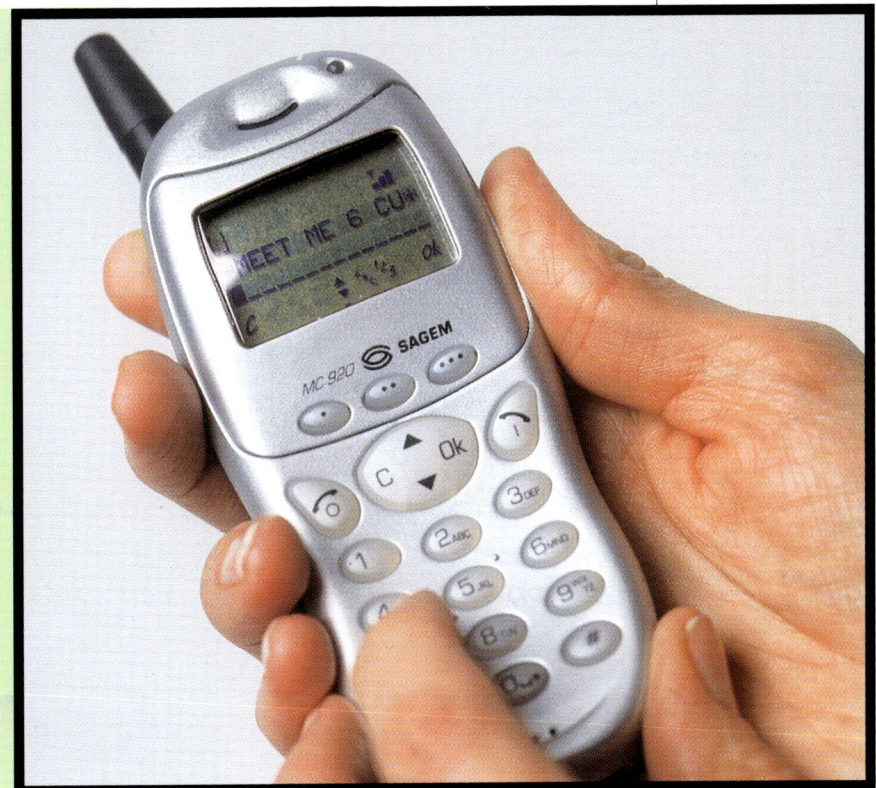

A Wireless Access Protocol (WAP) phone is a telephone that can send and receive e-mails. You write the e-mail using the numbered buttons.

E-mail addresses

Anybody who wants to send and receive e-mails needs their own e-mail address. This is the name of an electronic mailbox at a **server** computer, where e-mails sent to the person are stored.

All e-mail addresses look something like this:
myname@myserver.com

- 'myname' is the name of the person whose e-mail address it is.

- @ means 'at'.

- 'myserver' is the address of the server on the Internet, and is also called a domain name.

- '.com' tells you that the server is run by a commercial company.

To get an e-mail that has been sent to you, you have to look in your electronic mailbox. The e-mail is then moved from the box to your computer. It is a bit like going to a real postbox to collect the post! But just as you get unwanted mail through your real postbox, you can get 'junk' e-mails in your e-mail box. Think carefully about whom you give your e-mail address to.

SENDING AN E-MAIL

In most mail programs, the first stage in sending an e-mail is to select the 'New mail message' command. Then you enter the e-mail address of the person you are sending the message to, called a recipient. (The address might be stored in what is called the program's address book.) Then you fill in what the e-mail is about before writing the message itself. When the message is complete, you select the 'Send' command.

Into the Internet

When you select 'Send', the e-mail program puts the e-mail into its outbox, from where it sends it into the Internet. If you are **off-line**, the computer dials up your **Internet Service Provider** (ISP) before sending the e-mail.

Amazingly enough, the e-mail is not sent through the Internet in one piece. It is sent in small chunks called packets. Each packet contains some of the e-mail, together with information such as the address of the **server** it came from and the address of the server it is going to. These two servers are unlikely to be directly connected together, so the packets are passed from server to server until they arrive in the right place.

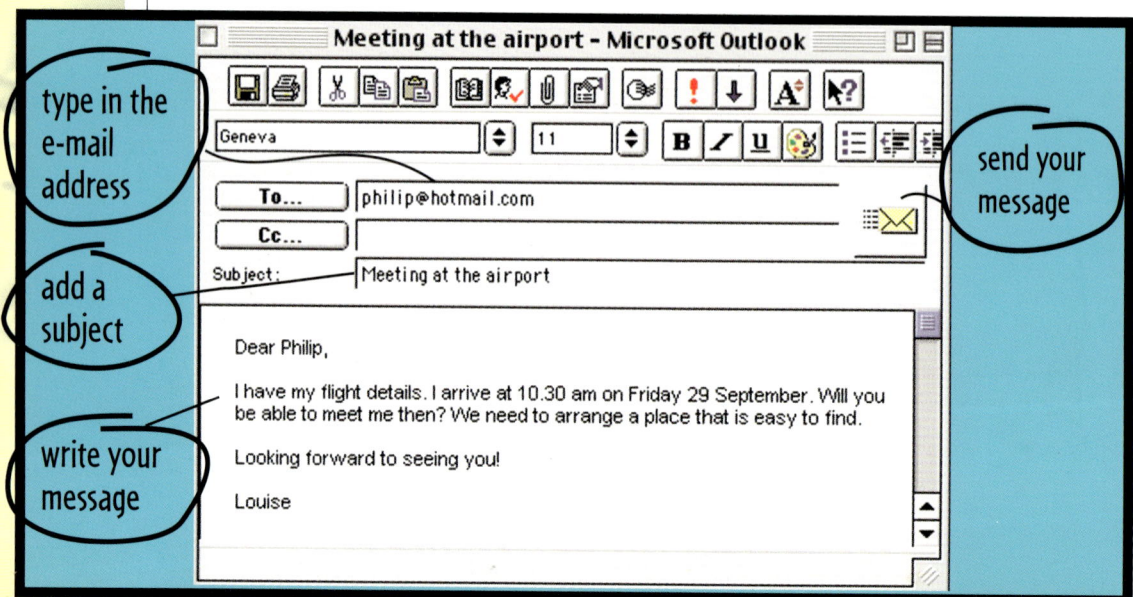

This computer screen shows you each stage of the process of writing and sending an e-mail. All you need to know is the e-mail address of the person you are writing to.

Which way?

The servers decide which is the quickest way to send each packet. Packets that are part of the same e-mail might even get to their destination by different routes! When they have all arrived at the final server, **software** on the server puts them back in order to make the e-mail. Then, it looks at the e-mail's address and puts it into the correct electronic **mailbox**, ready to be collected.

If the address on an e-mail is wrong, the e-mail will never arrive. Either the sender's server, or the final server, will send an e-mail back to whoever sent it to say that the address does not exist. If you are **on-line** and don't know a person's e-mail address, you can often find it using a **directory** on an Internet **search engine** (see page 20).

If you don't have a computer at home you can send e-mails and surf the **World Wide Web** at an Internet café or a library, like this one.

GETTING AN E-MAIL

If you access the Internet through an **Internet Service Provider** (ISP), you don't know when you have been sent an e-mail. The only way to find out is to look in your **mailbox** on the ISP's **server**. You can do this by selecting 'Get new mail' in your e-mail program. If you are **off-line**, the computer dials up the ISP first. Then, the computer sends the server your personal password, asks it to check your mailbox, and **downloads** any new messages so that you can read them. They appear in the inbox on your e-mail program.

People who are connected to the Internet through their office might see a 'You have new mail' message on their computer screens when e-mails arrive at the company's server.

E-mail from anywhere

Most Internet Service Providers use **POP mail**, which means that you can collect e-mail from any computer anywhere in the world. With **web mail**, you can send and receive e-mails via a **website**. This is useful for people who are on the move. They can use e-mail from anywhere they can get Internet access, such as an Internet café.

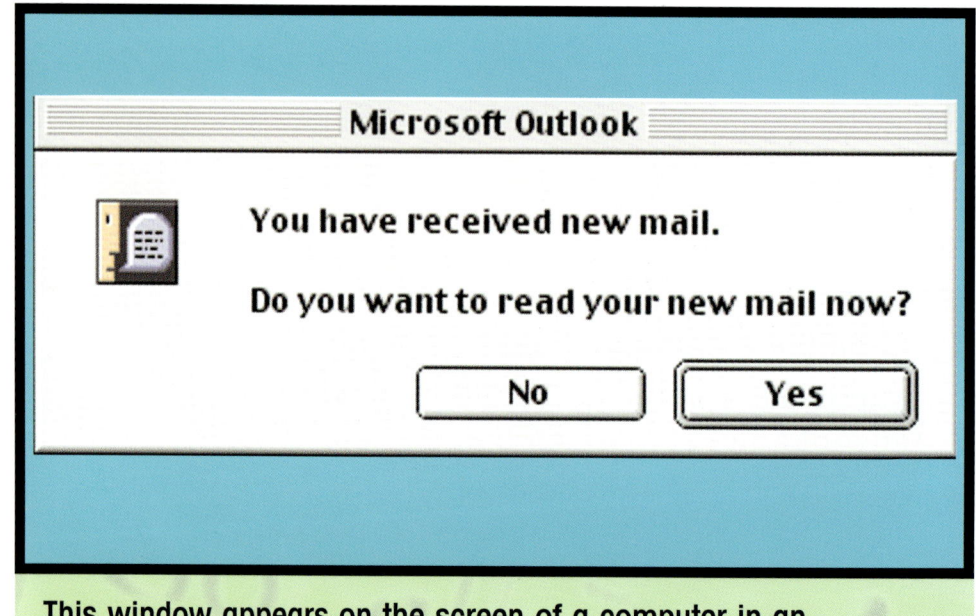

This window appears on the screen of a computer in an office if somebody sends an e-mail to the person working on the computer.

You can reply to an e-mail easily, by selecting 'Reply' in your e-mail program after reading the e-mail. The program gives you a new message box to fill in, with the address and subject already filled in.

Our example message has been collected from its mailbox. You can see how a reply is sent below. It includes an **attachment**, which is a picture **file** that shows a map of the airport, so that these two people can find each other there.

Viruses by e-mail

A virus is a program that secretly loads itself into your computer and often causes chaos. Viruses can be attached to e-mails, so it is important to be wary of opening attachments on e-mails from unknown people. E-mail viruses often send themselves to other people in your address list, too. Anti-virus **software** can warn of viruses arriving in your computer.

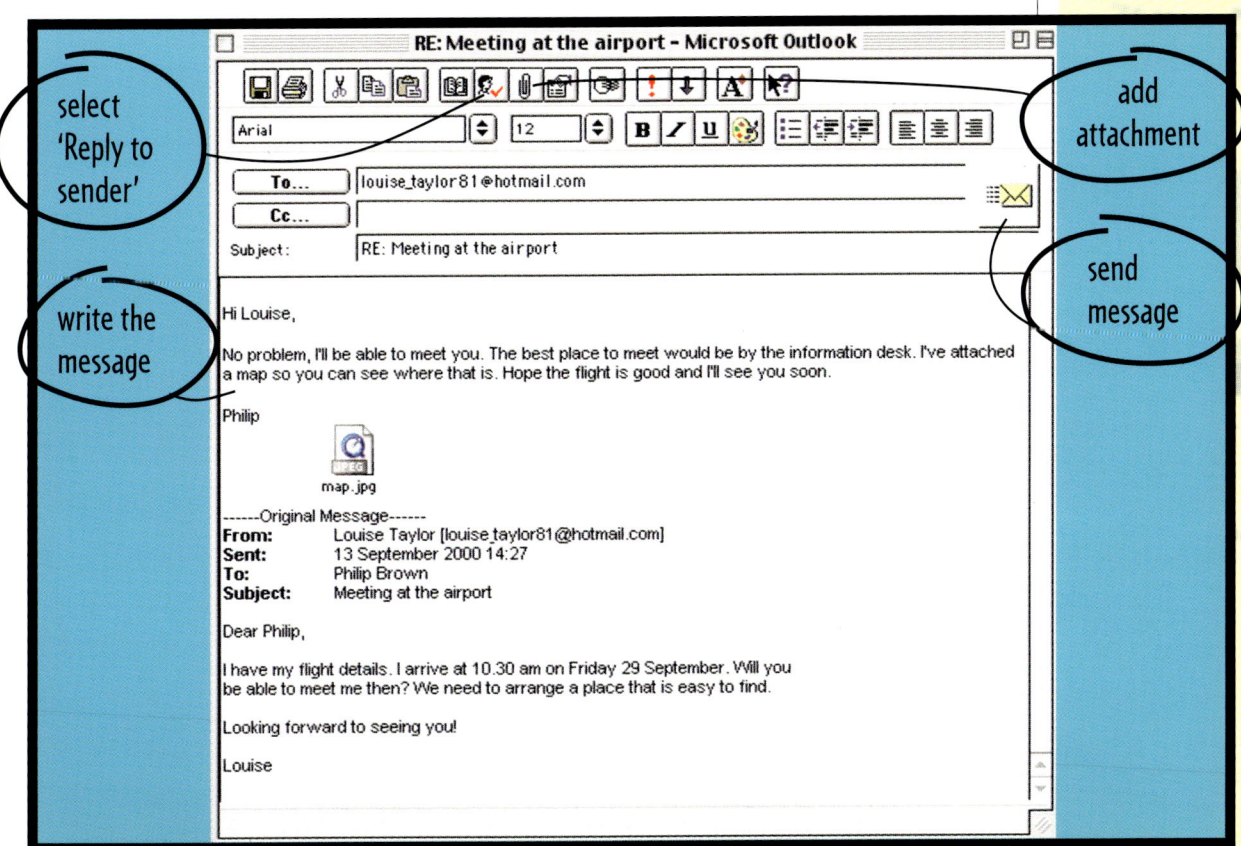

This screen shows you what you would see if you needed to reply to an e-mail. You type your reply above the original message.

THE WORLD WIDE WEB

People often think that the Internet and the **World Wide Web** are the same thing, but they are not. The Internet is a computer **network**. The World Wide Web (or just the Web, for short) is the name given to the huge collection of information that is stored on **servers** on the Internet. Anybody connected to the Internet can look at the information on the World Wide Web by copying it from the server to their own computer.

What's on the Web?

There is a staggering range of information on the Web, covering almost any subject you can think of – and probably many you can't! It is very useful for finding out things, perhaps for your hobby or for a homework project. Among many other things, the World Wide Web is used for **on-line** shopping, banking and finding out the news and weather.

It is worth remembering that anybody with a computer can put information on the Internet – and that information can be anything, even complete nonsense. Just because you read something on the Internet, it does not mean that it is true.

These children are looking at web pages on a computer at their school. They might be looking at pages on any one of millions of different subjects.

This is part of the website of WWF. This page tells you about the charity's campaigns and provides links to other pages.

Websites and web pages

The World Wide Web is made up of millions upon millions of pages of information, called **web pages**, which contain text, pictures, sounds and video clips. A **website** is a collection of web pages put together by a person or an organization.

Each website has its own Internet address, technically called a Uniform Resource Locator (URL), so that other computers know where to find it. For example, the URL of NASA's website is 'www.nasa.gov'.

When you visit a website, you move between the pages by clicking on hyperlinks (or just links). These are highlighted words or pictures that make your cursor turn into a hand when you point at them on a page. Clicking on a link takes you to another page, or a completely different website.

SURFING THE WEB

Looking at **websites** is known as 'surfing the Web'. To surf the Web, you need a connection to an **Internet Service Provider** (ISP), and a program on your computer called a web **browser**, such as Microsoft® Internet Explorer®. A browser program gets **web pages** from **servers** on the Internet and displays them on the computer screen. It also allows you to jump between web pages and websites.

What is where?

If you want to look at information on a website, or visit an **on-line** shop or bank (which is really a sophisticated website), you need its Internet address. Often, you will know the address anyway because you have visited the site before or seen it written down in an advert or magazine.

There are several browser programs available for computers. Make sure you choose the right one for your needs. This one is Netscape®, which is often used in offices.

This window shows the results from a search engine. The user entered the words 'space shuttle' for the search. Each heading is a different website.

If you are trying to find websites about certain subjects, or the website of a particular person or company, you need some help to find the addresses. The easiest place to find help is a website called a **search engine**, such as Google™ or AltaVista®. A search engine knows the addresses of millions of websites and what is stored on their pages. When you visit a search engine, you type in the subject you are interested in and the search engine sends you a list of websites that might be useful to you. Unfortunately, there are often thousands of suggestions to look at! If you click on the addresses of the sites, you will see the first page – normally an introductory page called a **home page**.

Can't find the site?

Sometimes you will get a message on your computer screen saying that the site you have tried to get into cannot be found. There are several reasons why this might happen. The address itself might be wrong, or the server might be switched off or 'down', meaning its **hardware** or **software** has a fault. Sometimes the site's pages are being redesigned.

THROUGH THE INTERNET

A **website** is really just a collection of computer **files** stored on a **server**. When you enter the address of a **web page** into your **browser** program, the browser sends a request for the page you want through the Internet to the server where the page is stored.

The server then sends the files that make up the page back through the Internet to your computer. As with e-mail, the files are broken down into small chunks called packets, each addressed to your computer. As they arrive, they are stored in the computer's memory. Live sound from Internet radio stations and live video from **web cameras** arrive as a stream of packets.

Generally, the more complicated the page that you are **downloading**, the longer it takes to download. Detailed moving pictures take longest. Most web browsers allow you to turn off pictures so that pages finish loading more quickly.

This is the picture from a web camera (or webcam) in the panda enclosure at San Diego Zoo in California. Anybody on the Internet can see the pictures from the camera.

Programming pages

The main file for a web page is called an **HTML** file (short for HyperText Markup Language). It is a computer language that contains the text that appears on the page, describes the colour and size of the text, the links from the page to other pages, the other files that are part of the page, and further details. Other files are for photographs, video and sounds that appear on the page. The HTML file tells the browser where and when they appear on the page.

The example web page from a browser on page 20 has an HTML file which includes the text, and additional files for the NASA logo, the photographs and the icons on the page.

Internet security

Any **data** that passes through the Internet can be read by other Internet users. So when people send information that they don't want others to see, such as a credit card number, it is important to connect through a 'secure' server. This puts the information into a code that would take years to break.

A Wireless Access Protocol (WAP) phone cannot show large web pages like a computer can. The pages are much simpler and made up mostly of text and small icons.

BUILDING A WEBSITE

Creating a collection of **web pages** on the Web for people to visit is called building a **website**. You don't need to understand Hypertext Markup Language (**HTML**) to build a website because there are web authoring programs that do the job for you. All you have to do is write the text and select photographs and other pictures to go on your pages. Large companies and organizations that have websites for information or **on-line** shopping employ web designers to build their websites. People called webmasters make sure that the site is working properly and that the information on it is up to date.

Step-by-step website

The first step in building a website, and probably the most important step, is deciding what information to put on it. If you are building one, remember that it is the contents of the site that are important as well as what it looks like.

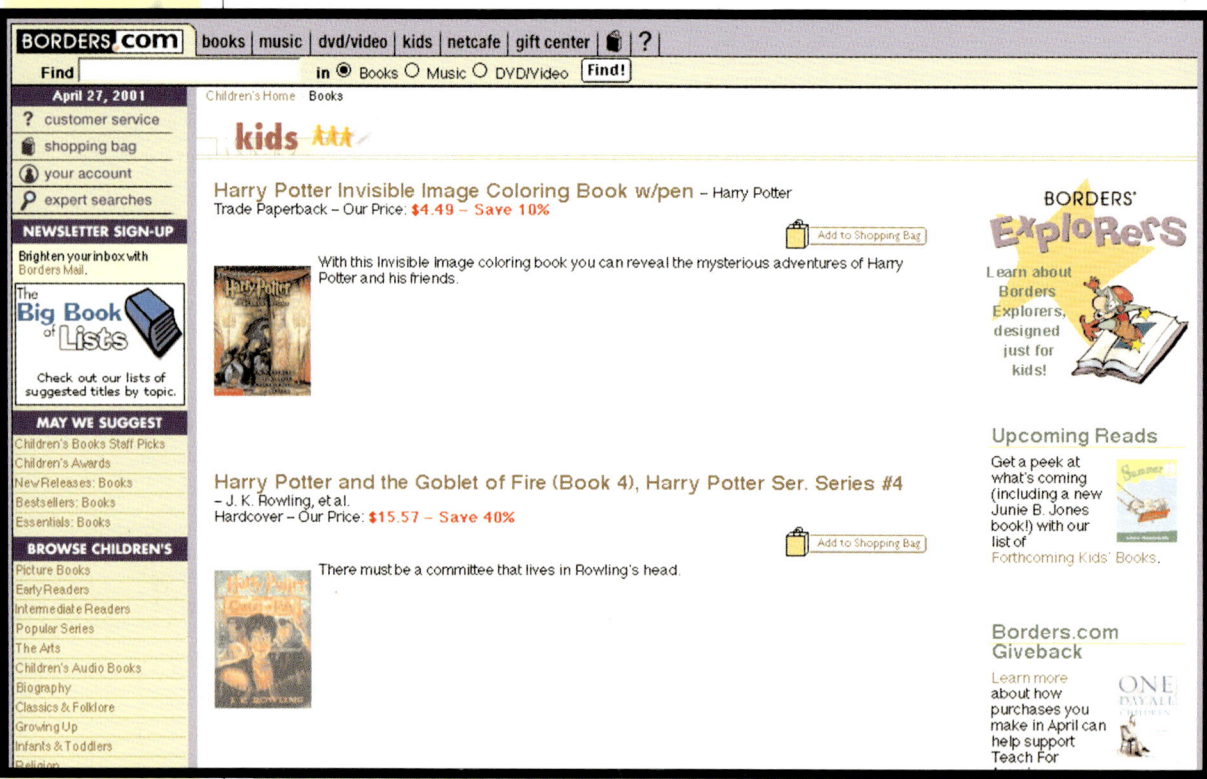

This is the website of a company that sells books. The list on left shows the different parts of the site you can visit.

This is the back of a **digital camera**. Most digital cameras can take pictures that you can put straight on to a website.

The next step is to decide how to divide the information into pages. If you were designing a website for your school, you might decide to include general information about the school (its name, address and so on), school news, school sports team results, photographs of the teachers and classes of pupils, information about the school play, and so on. It is important that your site is easy for people find their way (or navigate) around, so each page should have a link back to the **home page**.

Once you have decided how to organize your site, you can build it using a web authoring program. This lets you put text, pictures, and so on, on individual pages and create links between the pages. When all the pages are complete, you need to put copies of them on a **server** that is constantly connected to the Internet, so that people can visit the site at any time of the day. This is called **uploading** the site. You also need to get a web address, such as www.ourschool.com. If you want people to find your site as they are using the Internet, you need to put the address on the **directory** of at least one **search engine**.

INTERNET NEWS AND CHAT

E-mail and the **World Wide Web** are the main uses of the Internet, but they are not the only ones. You can also play games, join in with discussions about your favourite subject, chat with people using your computer, and get free **software**.

Newsgroups

A newsgroup is a group of Internet users who discuss their favourite topics over the Internet. There are tens of thousands of different newsgroups. If you have an unusual pet, there is probably a newsgroup dedicated to it! A newsgroup works like an electronic notice-board where messages are stored on a **server**. You can send a message to the newsgroup that all the other members of the group can read. You can also read messages that other members have sent.

Mailing lists are lists of e-mail addresses. An e-mail sent to a list goes to all the addresses on it. For example, you could join a weather forecast mailing list so that a weather forecast is e-mailed to you every morning.

The latest computer games consoles are equipped with **modems** and software so that they can be connected to the Internet. This allows people to play games against each other **on-line**.

Business meetings are cheaper thanks to Internet telephony and video conferencing. People no longer need to spend time and money travelling to meet each other.

Internet chat

An Internet chat room is a server on the Internet where people have conversations through their computers. Connecting to the server is like entering the chat room. People say things by typing messages on their keyboards, and the messages appear on the screens of everybody who is connected. The two most common systems are Web Chat, where you connect to a **website** to chat, and Internet Relay Chat (IRC), which is dedicated to chat. There are chat rooms for people interested in many subjects.

Net telephony and video conferencing

Two people connected to the Internet can talk to each other using Internet telephony. Each person needs a microphone attached to their computer. Their voices are turned into **files** that travel through the Internet to the other computer. Video conferencing allows two or more people to see and talk to each other using small cameras mounted on their computers.

INTERNET TIMELINE

Here are some of the major events and technical developments in the history of the Internet.

1940s   The first working computers are developed. They are so big that they fill whole rooms, but are only as powerful as a modern electronic calculator.

1947   The development of the transistor (an electronic switch) and, in 1959, the integrated circuit (or silicon chip) allows electronic circuits to be made far smaller.

late 1950s   The US Department of Defence sets up the Advanced Research Projects Agency (ARPA) in an attempt to keep up in the 'space race' with the Soviet Union.

1962   The age of global communication begins with the launch into orbit of the Telstar communications **satellite**.

1969   As a way of protecting its important research **data** from possible nuclear strikes, ARPA links together powerful computers at different sites to form ARPAnet, the forerunner of the Internet.

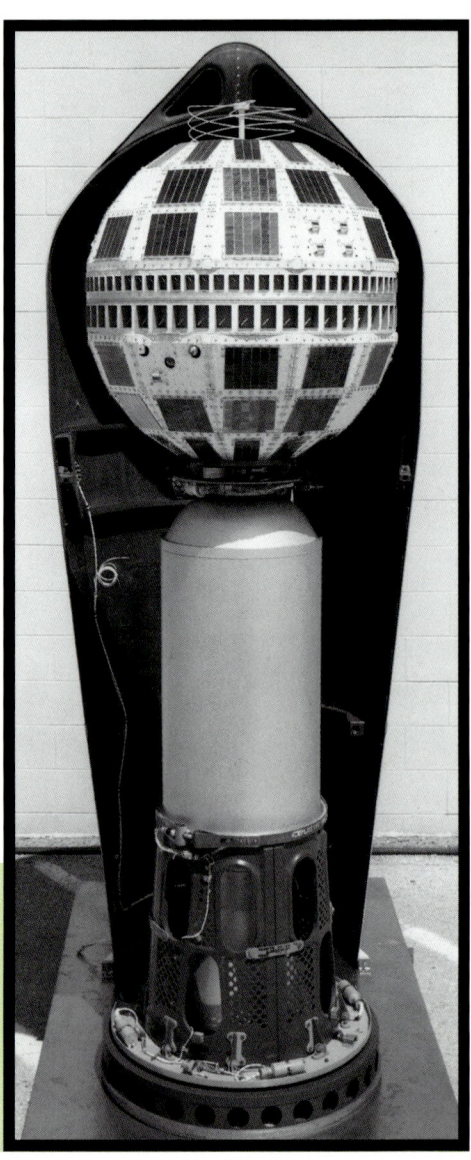

The Telstar communications satellite ready for launch inside a protective dome that was mounted on a rocket.

The Internet started as a way of keeping the United States' vital military data safe. The idea was developed here, at the Pentagon, headquarters of the US Department of Defence.

1970s American academic institutions, such as Harvard University, join ARPAnet, and begin using it to exchange messages. E-mail has been invented.

early 1980s Similar **networks** are created in other countries and join together with ARPAnet to create a worldwide computer network. More and more organizations join the network.

1989 The **World Wide Web** system of storing and retrieving information is devised. Many web **browsers** quickly appear.

mid-1990s Companies have begun to realize that the Internet can help them advertise their products and work more efficiently. Individuals are finally able to access the Internet through **Internet Service Providers**.

late 1990s Access to the Internet becomes possible through mobile phones and televisions.

2000 More than 300 million people are **on-line**.

GLOSSARY

ADSL short for Asynchronous Digital Subscriber Line – a high-speed digital telephone line

analogue describes a signal that is transmitted as a continuous wave and can have any strength

attachment file that is attached to an e-mail and travels with it

browser computer program that downloads and displays web pages

cable way of broadcasting by sending signals along underground cables

data any information stored on computer

digital 1) signal that is made up of on and off pulses of electricity, represented by the binary digits 0 and 1. 2) Any information stored in the form of the binary digits 0 and 1.

directory list of people, companies or organizations, sorted alphabetically or by function

download to copy a computer file from one computer to another computer

file collection of data stored in one place

hard drive data storage device in a computer, where data is stored magnetically on a solid disk

hardware physical parts of a computer, for example the monitor and keyboard

home page the first or title page of a website, normally the first one you see when you visit the site

HTML short for Hypertext Markup Language, the computer language used to describe a web page

infra-red links links in a computer network along which data travels as bursts of infra-red light

Internet Service Provider (ISP) organization that operates a server that allows people to access the Internet via their telephone lines

ISDN short for Integrated Services Digital Network, a type of high-capacity data link

kilobyte a measure of computer data, equal to 1024 bytes or 8192 individual bits (a bit is a zero or a one)

mailbox electronic postbox where e-mails are stored before they are collected

modem short for modulator/demodulator. It allows a digital computer to be attached to an analogue telephone line.

network two or more computers connected together so that they can share programs and data

off-line attached to, but not actually connected to, an ISP. Opposite of on-line.

on-line connected to an ISP

optical fibre thin fibre of glass that carries communications signals as pulses of light

personal digital assistant (PDA) electronic device that is a diary, notebook, address book and so on

POP mail short for Post Office Protocol, an e-mail system that allows users to collect e-mail from their mailboxes from any computer, anywhere in the world

satellite object that orbits around the Earth in space

search engine special website that searches for other websites that you might be interested in

server computer on a network that stores files that can be accessed by other computers on the network

software programs and data stored on a computer

upload copy a computer file from your own computer on to another, remote computer

web camera digital camera that Internet users can see through by visiting a website

web mail e-mail that is stored on a website and can be accessed from a browser

web page document that can be viewed by a web browser

website collection of web pages

Wireless Access Protocol (WAP) system that allows Internet access through a mobile phone

World Wide Web also known as the Web, a huge source of information that can be accessed by any computer on the Internet

INDEX

accessing the Internet 8–11
addresses
  e-mail 13, 14, 15
  Internet 19, 20, 21, 25
ADSL and ISDN lines 9
analogue signals 9

browsers 20, 22, 23

chat rooms 27
computers 5, 6–7, 10, 12
  hard drives 6
  servers 6, 7, 8, 13, 14, 15, 18, 20, 22, 23, 25, 26
  terminals 6
convergence 11

data 5, 6, 7, 8, 9, 10, 11, 23
dial-up connections 8
digital signals 9, 11
directories 15, 25
downloading 16, 22, 23

e-mail 5, 10, 12–17, 23, 26, 29
  addresses 13, 14, 15
  attachments 12, 17
  receiving 16-17
  replying to 17
  sending 14-15

files 22, 23, 27

games consoles 11, 26

history of the Internet 28–9
home pages 21, 25
HTML files 23
hyperlinks 19, 25
Hypertext Markup Language (HTML) 23, 24

infra-red links 7
Internet cafés 15, 16

Internet Service Providers (ISPs) 7, 8, 11, 14, 16, 20
Internet telephony 27

mailboxes 12, 13, 15, 16
mailing lists 26
modems 9, 10, 26

networks 6, 7, 18
newsgroups 26

on-line and off-line 8, 11, 14, 15, 16

POP mail 16

satellite links 7
search engines 15, 21, 25
security 23
software 10, 12, 15, 17, 21, 26
sound and video 22, 23
surfing the Web 15, 20

telephones 9, 10, 11, 23
television 11

Uniform Resource Locators (URLs) 19
uploading 25

video conferencing 27
viruses 17

web authoring programs 24, 25
web cameras 22
web mail 16
web pages 19, 20, 22, 23, 24
websites 19, 20, 21, 27
  building 24–5
Wireless Access Protocol (WAP) 10, 23
World Wide Web 5, 10, 18–25, 26, 29